A map in the

CW01668623

Story written by Cynthia Rider
Illustrated by Tim Archbold

Speed Sounds

Consonants

Ask children to say the sounds.

f	l	m	n	r	s	v	z	**sh**	**th**	**ng**
ff	ll	**mm**	nn	rr	ss	ve	zz			nk
	le		kn		ce		s			

b	c	d	g	h	j	p	qu	t	w	x	y	ch
bb	k	dd	gg			pp		tt	wh			**tch**
	ck											

Each box contains one sound but sometimes more than one grapheme.
Focus graphemes for this story are ***circled****.*

Vowels

Ask children to say the sounds in and out of order.

a	e ea	i	o	u	ay	**ee** y	igh	ow
at	hen	in	on	up	day	see	high	blow

oo	oo	ar	or	air	ir	ou	oy
zoo	look	car	for	fair	whirl	shout	boy

Story Green Words

Ask children to read the words first in Fred Talk and then say the word.

Zac Yasmin Grandad's map steep hill

past deep pond flock crack match

been sheep

Ask children to say the syllables and then read the whole word.

att|ic ver|y

Ask children to read the root first and then the whole word with the ending.

peep → peeps duck → ducks tree → trees

ticket → tickets week → week's

trick → tricking

Red Words

Ask children to practise reading the words across the rows, down the columns and in and out of order clearly and quickly.

we	to	he	they
go	are	of	for*
looks*	good*	the	was
what	you	I'll	your

** Red Word in this book only*

A map in the attic

Introduction
Have you ever followed a map? A map is a picture which tells you which way to go to get somewhere. In this story Zac and his sister Yasmin find a map in Grandad's attic – it tells them how to reach a big rock. What do you think they will find when they get there? Let's see what happens.

Zac and Yasmin see a green box in Grandad's attic.

Yasmin peeps in and sees a map.

Zac looks at the map.

"We must get to this big rock," he says.

They set off up a steep hill.

They go past a deep pond with six ducks swimming on it.

They go past a flock of sleepy sheep.

At last, they see a rock next to three trees.

Yasmin sees a tin in a crack in the rock.

In it are three tickets for next week's match!

"Grandad has been tricking us!" says Zac. "But it's a very good trick, Grandad!"

Questions to talk about

Ask children to TTYP for each question using 'Fastest finger' (FF) or 'Have a think' (HaT).

p.8	(FF)	What colour is the box in Grandad's attic?
	(FF)	What does Yasmin spot inside?
p.9	(FF)	Where does Zac think they must get to?
pp.10–11	(FF)	What do they go past?
p.12	(FF)	What does Yasmin spot? Where is it?
p.13	(HaT)	Who do you think hid the map in the attic?
	(HaT)	What does Zac think of the surprise?